# The
# Bald Eagle

Other titles in the Returning Wildlife series include:

Bats
The North American Beaver
North American River Otters

Returning Wildlife

# The Bald Eagle

John E. Becker

KIDHAVEN PRESS

THOMSON
™
GALE

*Detroit • New York • San Diego • San Francisco
Boston • New Haven, Conn. • Waterville, Maine
London • Munich*

*To my grandson Brandon, who is such a joy in my life.*

Library of Congress Cataloging-in-Publication Data

John E. Becker
  The Bald eagle / by John E. Becker.
    p. cm. — (Returning wildlife)
  Includes bibliographical references (p.    ).
Summary: Discusses the near extinction, return, and future
of bald eagles.
  ISBN 0-7377-1279-1 (hardback)
  1. Bald eagle—Juvenile literature. 2. Endangered species—
Juvenile literature. 3. Wildlife conservation—Juvenile literature.
[1. Bald eagle. 2. Eagles. 3. Endangered species. 4. Wildlife
conservation.] I. Title. II. Series.
  QL696.F32 B425 2002
  598.9'43—dc21

2001007842

Copyright 2002 by KidHaven Press,
an imprint of The Gale Group
10911 Technology Place, San Diego, CA 92127

Printed in the U.S.A.

# Contents

# chapter 1

# America's Eagle

Eagles have been admired throughout history for their size, power, and majestic appearance. They are related to other birds of prey (birds that hunt using specialized feet and beaks), such as hawks, falcons, and owls. Although eagles are widely distributed around the world, bald eagles are found only in North America.

When European settlers first arrived in North America, tens of thousands of bald eagles lived across the continent. The leaders of the United States chose the bald eagle as the country's national symbol out of respect for its strength and independence. Yet Americans have destroyed bald eagle habitat, polluted the water where bald eagles fish, and shot bald eagles as pests.

In the 1940s the United States passed laws to protect bald eagles because they were disappearing. Unfortunately, in that same decade a new threat to bald eagles, the deadly **pesticide DDT**, began to drastically reduce their numbers.

A bald eagle, symbol of strength and independence, soars high in the sky.

Further legal protection in the form of the Endangered Species Act, and the banning of DDT, started bald eagles on the road to recovery. Today, bald eagles are a source of national pride as an endangered species success story.

## Eagles Worldwide

The ancestors of today's eagles lived between 35 million and 50 million years ago. Their descendants in North America, bald eagles, have lived here for more than 1 million years.

Bald eagles are grouped with other birds of prey that hunt during the day in the scientific order Falconiformes. The bald eagle's scientific name, *Haliaeetus leucocephalus,* is taken from Greek words meaning "sea eagle, white headed." Bald eagles are considered sea eagles because they live near water and eat fish. Eight types of sea eagles live in all major parts of the world except Central and South America. Bald eagles are the only eagles that live exclusively in North America.

## Eagles Admired Throughout History

Eagles have long been a source of fascination ever since humans' earliest days on earth. In Europe, drawings of eagles that date back to the Stone Age have been found on the walls of caves. Eagles are mentioned in ancient mythology as "carriers of fire to mankind." The Bible refers to the strength and swiftness of eagles. And many ancient cultures, such as Babylon, Egypt, Persia, and Rome selected eagles as their national symbol.

In North America, some Native Americans believe that eagles are messengers between themselves and the creator. Because they viewed eagles as sacred animals, they usually killed them only to obtain their feathers for ceremonies.

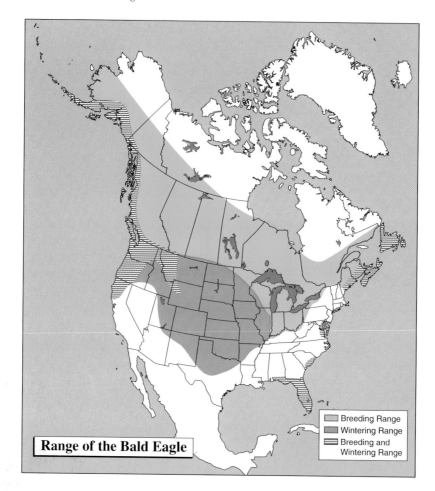

**Range of the Bald Eagle**

Breeding Range
Wintering Range
Breeding and Wintering Range

## The Role of Bald Eagles in Nature

Bald eagles and other birds of prey are called **raptors.** Raptors are the top predators among birds. As airborne hunters, bald eagles are ideally equipped to capture and kill prey. They have four toes on each foot with powerful claws called **talons**. Three toes point forward and one backward giving them a vicelike grip. When an eagle strikes a fish or other animal the talons sink in deeply, ensuring that the prey will not escape.

The eagle then flies its meal to a **perch** to eat. Because it has no teeth, the eagle uses its large, hooked beak to tear the prey into bite-sized pieces that it swallows whole. Bald eagles are quick to consume a meal, finishing a one-pound fish in just four minutes.

Bald eagles prefer to eat fish, but they will also eat birds such as ducks and geese. Small mammals, including rabbits, squirrels, prairie dogs, opossums, and raccoons are eaten by bald eagles as well.

Unfortunately, many farmers have a strong dislike for bald eagles. Farmers often mistakenly believe bald eagles eat sheep and other domestic livestock. Although bald eagles will occasionally eat domestic animals, they more often eat animals such as rabbits. Because rabbits eat crops, bald eagles are actually helpful to farmers.

A juvenile bald eagle grasps a snow goose in its vicelike talons.

**Carrion** (dead animals) is another important food source for bald eagles. Dead fish and road-killed deer, for example, are favorite food items. By eating carrion, bald eagles help to maintain a clean, disease-free environment.

A bald eagle guards its next meal—a dead caribou.

## Bald Eagle Facts

Bald eagles are the second-largest raptors in North America; only California condors are larger. A male bald eagle may stand two and a half feet tall, weigh ten pounds, and have a wingspan of six feet. Females are one-third larger than males (female raptors generally are larger than males). Females may stand three feet tall, weigh fourteen pounds, and have a wingspan of seven and a half feet. Their distinguishing feature, the white feathers that cover their heads, do not appear until the eagle is four or five years old.

The most important sense for an eagle is its keen sight. A bald eagle's vision is three times greater than a person's. There are several reasons for the difference. First, the eyes of a bald eagle are quite large in relation to the size of its head. That gives the eagle a large surface area on the retina (the inner surface of the eye) where visual images are recorded. Second, the eagle's eye has five times as many **photoreceptors** (light-sensitive cells) as a person's eye. This allows the eagle to see things in much greater detail. Bald eagles also have foveas, two areas in their eyes in which images are concentrated. A lateral fovea gives an eagle greater vision to the side of its head, and a temporal fovea gives an eagle better forward vision. Humans have only one fovea in each eye.

Bald eagles also have better color vision than humans. People have the ability to see three basic colors; blue, green, and red. The human brain transforms those three colors into the variety of colors that people see. But bald eagles can see five basic colors, which allows them to see very slight differences in colors. That is why eagles can distinguish an animal from its surroundings at great distances. An eagle for example, can see a fish underwater from one hundred feet above, or spot a rabbit against a dark background from a mile away.

Bald eagles' other senses are not as well developed as their sense of sight. Their ability to hear, for example, is about the same as a person's, while their sense of smell and taste are poorer than a person's.

Large wings, hollow, air-filled bones, and powerful flight muscles allow bald eagles to fly. But they rely on their ability to glide to stay aloft. The eagle's large wings

With wings spread wide, a bald eagle glides to stay aloft.

are ideal for gliding but make taking off and landing more difficult. A bald eagle must also use a great deal of energy to lift itself into the air. Once it finds an air draft, the eagle **soars** without flapping its wings while scanning the landscape below for prey.

## Raising the Young

An eagle's most spectacular flying takes place during courtship encounters. When a male and female join together at about four or five years of age, they usually nest together for life. The site they choose for their new nest is a typical bald eagle habitat. They look for tall trees, or an area with high cliffs that offers a good view of the surrounding countryside. The site also includes a body of water that is well stocked with fish.

Once the nest is built, each year the pair will return to the same nest and make it larger. Some nests have been in use for more than sixty years. Nests that are fifteen feet high and ten feet across are not unusual. The nest is not built to hold a large family, however.

Female bald eagles will lay usually one, two, or in rare instances, three eggs. Both parents will take turns sitting on the eggs until they hatch. Newborn bald eagles are covered with a soft, gray **down**.

Bald eagle chicks grow quickly, and within a few weeks they are covered with a second coat of darker down. From three weeks to ten weeks, the chicks have hearty appetites and grow very rapidly. They eagerly gobble down scraps of food brought to the nest by their mother and father.

Between eleven and twelve weeks of age, young eaglets will take their first flights. Within a few weeks they are experienced flyers and ready to go off on their own. Once a young bald eagle is able to fly, it will leave its parents and seek the company of other young eagles.

A down-covered chick explores its nest.

## Surviving Winter

In the fall, as temperatures drop, some bald eagles will escape the cold northern weather and fly to warmer areas. Other bald eagles may stay in the cold weather all winter. Many bald eagles die during their first winter, because they are inexperienced hunters and may not find enough food to survive. But those that do survive may live over twenty-five years. Unfortunately, during the twentieth century, most bald eagles struggled to survive into adulthood.

# chapter 2

# Disappearance

**B**ald eagles are more vulnerable than other species of birds for several reasons. Because they are large birds with distinctive white feathers on their heads, hunters can spot them more easily. Bald eagles' habit of feeding on carrion also makes them easy to poison and trap. And when bald eagles eat fish, they may become victims of poisoning from pesticides such as DDT. These factors, and the destruction of their habitat, caused bald eagles to almost disappear in the lower forty-eight states during the twentieth century.

## Natural Enemies

Other animals occasionally prey on bald eagles. Adults are rarely attacked, but eggs and defenseless chicks are in danger if left unattended. Raccoons, bobcats, bears, and wolverines will rob eagle nests if given the opportunity. Some birds, such as gulls and crows, will also take eagle eggs. These and other animals may prey on eagles from time to time,

An adult bald eagle is easily identified by the white feathers covering its head.

but no animal poses a threat to the entire bald eagle species. Only humans have killed bald eagles in great enough numbers to drive them near extinction.

## Humans and Bald Eagles

Native Americans treated bald eagles with great respect but also killed them for ceremonies and for their feathers. Cheyenne warriors, for example, could kill an eagle to obtain its feathers, but only after performing a set of rituals. The warrior could not shed the eagle's blood, and could not use a weapon. He had to demonstrate his bravery by killing the eagle with his bare hands.

Other Native Americans used the talons of a bald eagle as part of a necklace that protected the wearer from evil spirits. Eagle bones and other parts were also used, but the feathers were the most prized part of the eagle.

Some tribes believed that eagle feathers had magical powers. Feathers were used to decorate clothing, headdresses, pipes, and shields. Each feather represented a courageous deed, and the wearing of many eagle feathers indicated an honored warrior.

Although it was common practice for Native Americans to kill eagles, there is no evidence that they caused bald eagle populations to drop significantly. Therefore, when Europeans first arrived in North America, they found a healthy population of between 250,000 and 500,000 bald eagles.

As Europeans settled in North America, they cut down trees to clear land for farming. Many of those were the tall, older trees that bald eagles prefer for their nests. As the settlers spread westward, they cleared increasingly larger areas. Over time, a great deal of the nesting habitat for bald eagles disappeared. Habitat destruction led to a decline in the bald eagle population, but other factors played an even greater role in their disappearance.

Since colonial times, farmers believed bald eagles killed their livestock. Bald eagles' habit of eating carrion has, no doubt, contributed to that belief. When predators kill farm animals, or when they die of natural causes, bald eagles will feed on the carcass. Farmers, therefore, assume that the eagle killed the animal. To protect their livestock, farmers shoot the offending eagle and any other eagle they see.

For many years, bald eagles were considered such a serious threat that several states offered **bounties** for killing them. In Alaska between 1917 and 1952, a bounty was offered for killing bald eagles. During that time, more than 128,000 were killed.

Through the years, thousands of bald eagles have also been shot for sport. As early as 1668 residents of Maine boasted about shooting dozens of bald eagles. In many parts of the country, hunters gathered on mountaintops to shoot migrating eagles as they flew overhead. Sport hunting of bald eagles continued well into the twentieth century.

Untold numbers of bald eagles have been poisoned. In some instances, farmers or ranchers poisoned fish or meat with the intent of killing bald eagles. At other times, bald eagles eat poisoned food intended for other pests.

Bald eagle feathers decorate a headdress belonging to an honored warrior.

Unregulated hunting once posed a serious threat to the bald eagle.

Many bald eagles have been killed in traps set for them or for other animals. A dead animal will attract an eagle to a trap. Once caught, few eagles escape.

The combination of loss of habitat, shooting, poisoning, and trapping took a heavy toll on the bald eagle population. By the middle of the twentieth century, people began to realize that a bald eagle was a rare sight in most of the lower forty-eight states. (There are no bald eagles in Hawaii and bald eagle populations in Alaska have remained healthy.) Just as the U.S. government began to take action to protect bald eagles, however, an even deadlier threat began to send their numbers dropping to critically low levels.

## DDT

In 1947 a chemical known as DDT began to be widely used in the United States as a pesticide to control insects that transmitted diseases, destroyed crops, or damaged trees. At that time, when DDT proved successful in killing harmful insects, people began spraying it on swamps, trees, farms, and in cities from coast to coast. In 1951, 106 million pounds of DDT were produced for use across the country.

Unfortunately, mosquitoes and other insects soon developed **immunity** to DDT. Animals higher in the food chain were not as fortunate. DDT accumulates in higher animals and is passed along to predators that eat those animals. When fish ate insects sprayed with DDT, large amounts of the pesticide accumulated in the fish. Thereafter, when a bald eagle ate fish with large amounts of DDT in their systems, the bald eagle suffered DDT poisoning.

In birds, DDT can kill chicks. Many bald eagle chicks died shortly after birth. DDT may also reduce the amount of calcium produced by female eagles, causing

A farmer sprays DDT on his crops. DDT traveled up the food chain, poisoning eagle chicks.

their eggs to have extremely thin shells. When eagles sat on the weakened eggs, they broke. Bald eagles were able to lay eggs, but very few chicks survived.

## Desperate Situation

The damaging effects of DDT were so widespread that observers noticed a dramatic decline in bald eagles during the 1960s. By 1970 it was estimated that only one

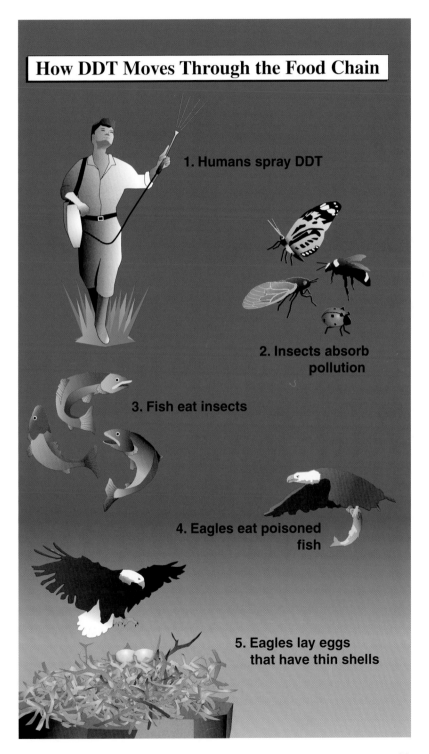

# How DDT Moves Through the Food Chain

1. Humans spray DDT

2. Insects absorb pollution

3. Fish eat insects

4. Eagles eat poisoned fish

5. Eagles lay eggs that have thin shells

A bald eagle swoops down to catch a fish.

thousand bald eagles were successfully breeding throughout the lower forty-eight states. At that time, Americans became aware that the nation's symbol was rapidly approaching extinction. The situation for bald eagles was desperate, but many people were determined to save them.

# chapter 3

# Bald Eagle Restoration

O nce people discovered why bald eagles were disappearing, steps were taken to restore the species to healthy population levels. The first step was to provide legal protection. Thereafter, laws were passed that made it illegal to kill bald eagles or destroy their habitat. When DDT was found to cause the death of bald eagle chicks, it was banned.

By the 1970s saving bald eagles from extinction became a popular cause around which governmental agencies, private conservation organizations, and individuals rallied together. Through their efforts, bald eagle numbers began to increase.

## Laws to Protect Eagles

In 1840 pioneer naturalist John James Audubon noted that bald eagles were declining in numbers along the Ohio and Mississippi Rivers. Years later, in 1876, breeding pairs of bald eagles were rare

Conservationists try to net a captive bald eagle.

in Illinois. By 1897 bald eagles were no longer nesting in Indiana. As the twentieth century dawned, fewer and fewer bald eagles could be found in the lower forty-eight states.

In an attempt to reverse the decline of bald eagles and other birds, the U.S. government approved a treaty to protect migratory birds that were common to Canada, Japan, Mexico, the Soviet Union, and America. The Migratory Bird Treaty Act of 1918 gave full protection to all migratory birds including their eggs, feathers, and nests.

Despite the protection afforded by the Migratory Bird Treaty Act, bald eagles continued to decline in numbers. Congress, recognizing the need for further legal help for bald eagles, passed the Bald Eagle Protection Act in 1940. That act made it illegal to kill, harass, or own a bald eagle.

## Identifying the Problem

From 1939 until 1959 Charles Broley conducted a study that revealed a dramatic decline in the number of bald eagles in Florida. Adult eagles were nesting, but few chicks were surviving. To determine the cause, bald eagle eggs were analyzed at the U.S. Fish and Wildlife Service's Patuxent Wildlife Research Center in Maryland. The center found that the eggs were extremely thin because of the effects of DDT. But was this just an isolated problem in Florida?

Observers at the Hawk Mountain Sanctuary in eastern Pennsylvania provided the answer. They had conducted yearly bald eagle counts since 1934. By the late 1950s their figures indicated a steady decline in bald eagle numbers. Their information confirmed that the drop-off in bald eagle populations was widespread. It was an alarming situation, but few people were aware of the extent of the problem.

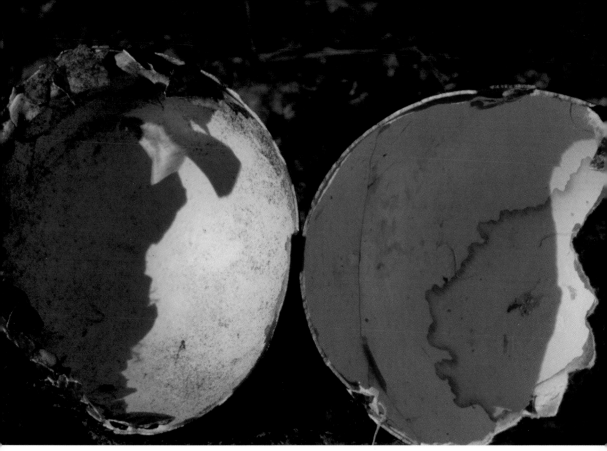

Thin eagle eggshells show signs of poisoning from DDT.

In 1962 biologist Rachel Carson published a book entitled *Silent Spring*. The book publicized the deadly effects of DDT on bald eagles and other animals. The resulting public outcry led to the United States banning DDT in 1972. The hard work and determination of many individuals and organizations was beginning to help bald eagles recover.

In 1973 the Endangered Species Act became law. Under that act, bald eagles and their habitat were protected in the lower forty-eight states.

During the 1970s and 1980s, 120 bald eagles died of lead poisoning in the United States. Recognizing this problem, beginning in 1986 the federal government outlawed the use of lead shot for waterfowl hunting. Waterfowl hunters now must use shot made of steel.

Environmentalist Rachel Carson's book *Silent Spring* publicized the harmful effects of DDT.

Native Americans are not exempt from laws protecting bald eagles. Because many tribes still use eagle feathers for ceremonies, however, they may obtain feathers from the U.S. government. Dead bald eagles are turned over to the U.S. Fish and Wildlife Service and they issue permits to Native Americans allowing them to obtain feathers from the dead eagles.

Despite laws to protect them, bald eagles continued to disappear until Broley's important discovery helped them recover.

## Organizations Helping Bald Eagles

The list of organizations that have helped restore bald eagles is extensive. A few of those organizations deserve special mention, however.

The U.S. Fish and Wildlife Service was created in 1940. Part of that agency's mission has been the protection of migratory birds, including bald eagles. The agency has purchased land for bald eagle preserves, analyzed toxic chemicals to determine their effect on bald eagles, and enforced endangered species laws that protect bald eagles.

The U.S. Department of Agriculture Forest Service has played a major role in protecting bald eagle habitat. Hundreds of thousands of acres across the country are

A bald eagle lies helplessly on the ground, its wing broken.

protected by the Forest Service as safe areas for nesting bald eagles.

Private organizations, such as The Nature Conservancy, have raised millions of dollars to purchase land for bald eagle sanctuaries. Those sanctuaries have been invaluable in providing habitat for growing bald eagle populations.

The National Wildlife Federation has also purchased land to establish bald eagle sanctuaries. In addition, that organization played a major role in outlawing the use of lead shot. The National Wildlife Federation also sponsored bald eagle counts nationwide for several years.

## Bald Eagle Comeback

One key element in the return of bald eagles was the establishment of federal and state "Recovery Plans" for the species. In many cases, those plans included innovative strategies to help bald eagles come back.

In 1976 the state of New York used a release strategy called **hacking**. Bald eagle chicks were brought from wild nests in Wisconsin, Michigan, Minnesota, and Alaska. The chicks, from six to nine weeks old, were then placed in man-made nest boxes. The boxes were mounted on "hacking towers" high above the ground where they were fed by hidden caretakers. At twelve weeks of age, when flight feathers were fully developed, the eaglets were released. From 1976 to 1988, 198 bald eagles were released in New York by this method.

Oklahoma used a different strategy with equally successful results. Bald eagle eggs were obtained from wild nests in Florida. The eggs were taken from the nests early enough in the breeding season that most of the bald eagles produced a second **clutch** (set) of eggs.

A bald eagle chick is weighed as part of a program to reintroduce healthy eagles to the wild.

The eggs that were removed were taken to Oklahoma and hatched in **incubators** at the George Miksch Sutton Avian Research Center. Thereafter, the Oklahoma-raised bald eagles were released in Alabama, Georgia, Mississippi, North Carolina, and Oklahoma. A total of 275 eagles were released through this program, which played a major role in reestablishing bald eagle populations in the southeastern United States.

Ohio used yet another strategy with good results called fostering. Bald eagles at three institutions, the Cincinnati Zoo, the Cleveland Museum of Natural History, and the Columbus Zoo, successfully hatched and raised chicks. Those chicks were released into the wild beginning in 1979. There were only four breeding pairs of bald eagles in the wild in Ohio that year. By the end of 2001 there were seventy-three breeding pairs in Ohio.

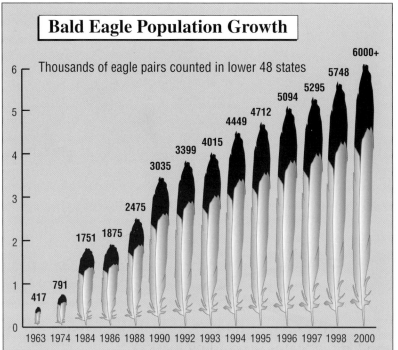

**Bald Eagle Population Growth**

Thousands of eagle pairs counted in lower 48 states

| Year | Value |
|------|-------|
| 1963 | 417 |
| 1974 | 791 |
| 1984 | 1751 |
| 1986 | 1875 |
| 1988 | 2475 |
| 1990 | 3035 |
| 1992 | 3399 |
| 1993 | 4015 |
| 1994 | 4449 |
| 1995 | 4712 |
| 1996 | 5094 |
| 1997 | 5295 |
| 1998 | 5748 |
| 2000 | 6000+ |

Source: U.S. Fish and Wildlife Service.

A bald eagle prepares to land by stretching out its legs.

As a result of restoration projects during the past thirty years, bald eagles have made an amazing recovery. In 1963 there were only 417 pairs of bald eagles surviving in the lower forty-eight states. Current estimates indicate that more than 6,000 pairs live across the United States (excluding Alaska).

A bald eagle spots a fish it wants to catch.

## Conservation Success Story

The return of bald eagles has been hailed as one of the greatest triumphs for wildlife conservation in America. In 1999 President Bill Clinton announced that bald eagles had recovered so well that the government proposed removing them from the Endangered Species List. The future for bald eagles is hopeful, but potential problems still exist.

# chapter 4

# A Bright Future

The gentleman holding the large bird cradled it gently in his arms. The bird's fierce yellow eyes and distinctive white head were unmistakably those of a bald eagle.

As the eagle looked on, the master of ceremonies addressed the sizable crowd. "Are you ready?" he asked.

Children excitedly leaned forward to get a better look.

"On the count of three . . . One . . . Two . . . *Three!*"

On three, the man holding the eagle hurled it into the air.

Immediately, it began flapping its long wings as it climbed higher and higher.

The people in the crowd rose in a chorus of cheers as the bird soared out of sight.

Those in the audience were witnessing an important event— the return of an injured bald eagle to the wild.

Several weeks before, the eagle had been shot and almost died. But concerned people brought it to The Raptor Center on the campus of the

A wildlife ranger prepares to return a rehabilitated juvenile bald eagle to the wild.

University of Minnesota. The staff and volunteers of the center spent countless hours mending the bird's shattered bones, caring for it as it recovered, and helping it to regain the strength it would need to fly again. Now their efforts were rewarded as the eagle joined many other injured raptors that have been returned to their natural habitat.

## Threats Still Remain

The restoration of bald eagles across the country has been a great success, but bald eagles still face a number of serious threats to their survival:

- As the human population grows, more and more wild areas are being converted into housing developments, business sites, and recreational areas. Human expansion also increases the demand for trees to supply the wood needed in building projects. If bald eagle habitat continues to disappear at the current rate, America's symbol may be in trouble again one day.

- Although DDT has been outlawed since 1972, other pesticides continue to pose a threat. Many types of pesticides are used across the United States each year. Scientists have not determined the long-term effects those chemicals may have on bald eagles.

- Other types of chemical pollutants are emptied into American waterways daily. Fish absorb the toxic material and pass it along when they are eaten by eagles. One day, those poisons may prove to be as deadly to bald eagles as DDT.

- Despite laws that make it a crime to kill bald eagles, many eagles are still shot to protect domestic animals. In some western states, ranchers defy the law and shoot eagles they believe are a threat to their livestock.

- Some people still shoot bald eagles for sport, or to make money from the sale of their feathers. When the state of Indiana released seventy-three young bald eagles from 1985 through 1989, five were shot.

- Power lines crisscross America from coast to coast. Those electric wires are a hazard for bald eagles. Each year, many bald eagles die from collisions with the wires, or from electrocution.

Collisions with power lines or electrocution from them kill many eagles each year.

• A growing number of bald eagles die when hit by cars. When an eagle feeds on road-killed animals, it runs the risk of being hit. The state of Ohio lists road-killed deaths as one of the major causes of bald eagle losses in that state.

Although there are still threats to bald eagles, they have not been left unprotected.

## Continued Legal Protection

Once they are removed from the Endangered Species List what legal protection will prevent bald eagles from becoming endangered again? The Endangered Species Act requires that the status of a species be checked for at least five years after the species has recovered. During that time, the federal government, in cooperation with the states, will have the responsibility of determining the population health of bald eagles. If they decline in numbers, they would quickly be added to the list again.

Bald eagles also continue to be protected under the Migratory Bird Treaty Act and the Bald and Golden Eagle Protection Act. Under these acts, it is still a crime to kill or possess eagles and their eggs, parts, or nests except under certain conditions (such as Native Americans obtaining bald eagle feathers for ceremonies). Bald eagles, therefore, will be protected as long as these laws remain in effect.

Continuing protection of nesting sites will also be crucial to maintaining healthy bald eagle populations in the future. The U.S. Fish and Wildlife Service maintains the 93 million acre National Wildlife Refuge System made up of more than five hundred national wildlife refuges across the country. Maintaining suitable bald

A bald eagle rests in its nest in an area protected by the National Wildlife Refuge System.

eagle habitat, including nesting sites, is one of the goals of the refuge system.

## People Assisting Bald Eagles

One of the most important ways in which people are helping bald eagles is by caring for injured eagles and returning those eagles to the wild whenever possible. The Raptor Center of the University of Minnesota is one of many **raptor rehabilitation facilities** across the country that gives medical assistance to injured birds. The Raptor Center has rehabilitated more than fifteen hundred bald eagles since 1974. Most bald eagles that are brought to The Raptor Center have been shot, caught in traps, poisoned, or hit by cars. It may take months of extensive treatment by veterinarian staff before injuries heal and a disabled bald eagle can be returned to the wild.

The future for bald eagles will depend, to a great extent, on people across the country keeping an accurate count of their numbers. Each year thousands of volunteers spend hundreds of thousands of hours observing bald eagles. Any drop in population, therefore, should be noted before the species declines to dangerously low levels again.

A band is placed on a bald eagle's ankle. The band allows researchers to track the bird and study its habits.

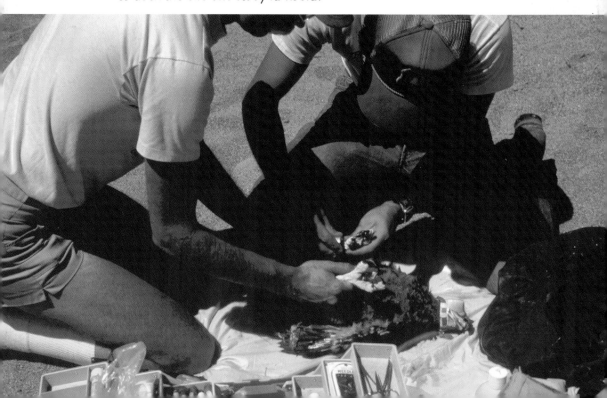

Observation and protection of the bald eagle will ensure its place in the wild.

Observing an eagle nest to determine the success or failure of a nesting pair of bald eagles provides important information for scientists studying bald eagles. In many locations around the United States, wildlife biologists have installed video cameras, called eagle cams, to observe an eagle nest on a continual basis.

Children are also helping bald eagles. Children in Ohio are volunteering at wildlife rehabilitation centers by cleaning cages and observing injured birds. In Wisconsin, schools have raised money in fund-raising

39

projects to "adopt" eagle nests. And the state of Illinois has distributed finger puppets for youngsters to color so that they can accurately spot bald eagles in their areas.

## Bald Eagles Soaring Across America

The story of the restoration of bald eagles across the United States is an exciting chapter in humankind's efforts to preserve the natural world. Hopefully, the bald eagle will continue to be a living symbol of America for generations to come.

**bounties:** Money paid for the killing of animal pests.

**carrion:** Flesh of a dead animal.

**clutch:** The number of eggs produced at one time.

**DDT:** Dichlorodiphenyltrichloroethane, a chemical compound used to kill insects.

**down:** A soft, fluffy covering of feathers.

**hacking:** A system of raising birds of prey by humans until the birds are capable of flying and hunting on their own.

**immunity:** An internal resistance to disease.

**incubator:** A machine that keeps eggs warm until they hatch.

**perch:** A high place on a tree or cliff from which an eagle may rest, eat, or hunt.

**pesticide:** A chemical used to kill pests such as insects.

**photoreceptors:** Light-sensitive cells known as rods and cones that are part of the inner surface of the eye (retina).

**raptor:** A bird that hunts and kills its prey using specialized feet and beaks.

**raptor rehabilitation facility:** A center where injured raptors are given medical treatment.

**soar:** To glide on a current of air.

**talons:** The long, curved claws of an eagle.

## Books and Periodicals

Karen Dudley, *Bald Eagles.* Austin, TX: Raintree Steck-Vaughn Publishers, 1998. In-depth look at bald eagles, their physical characteristics, behaviors, and endangerment.

H. Josef Hebert, "Bald Eagle Is off the Endangered List," *Yahoo! News,* June 17, 1999. Traces the decline of bald eagles across the United States and the steps taken for the species to recover.

Sylvia A. Johnson, *Raptor Rescue! An Eagle Flies Free.* New York: Dutton Children's Books, 1995. A behind-the-scenes look at a raptor rehabilitation facility.

Gordon Morrison, *Bald Eagle.* Boston: Houghton Mifflin, 1998. A nicely illustrated book focusing on the life cycle of bald eagles from chick to adulthood.

Dorothy Hinshaw Patent, *The Bald Eagle Returns.* New York: Clarion Books, 2000. The story of how America's symbol was rescued from the brink of extinction by concerned human beings.

Hope Ryden, *America's Bald Eagle.* New York: G.P. Putnam's Sons, 1985. Classic story of bald eagle development by one of America's premier nature writers.

## Organizations to Contact

Hawk Mountain Sanctuary
1700 Hawk Mountain Rd.
Kempton, PA 19529-9449
(610) 756-6000
website: www.hawkmountain.org

Raptor conservation organization located in eastern Pennsylvania.

The Raptor Center
University of Minnesota
Gabbert Raptor Building
1920 Fitch Ave.
St. Paul, MN 55108
(612) 624-4745
website: www.raptor.cvm.umn.edu

This organization rehabilitates injured raptors, including bald eagles.

## Websites

American Bald Eagle Information
www.baldeagleinfo.com

This site provides a wealth of information about bald eagles and their lore.

National Wildlife Federation
www.nwf.org/wildalive/eagle/index.html

This excellent site provides educational information about bald eagles.

## Videos

*Audubon's Animal Adventures: Eagle Adventures.* HBO Kids Video: National Audubon Society, 1997. Family video about bald eagles, their physical characteristics, behaviors, and the people who help injured eagles.

*Eagles: The Master of the Skies.* PBS Home Video: British Broadcasting Corporation, 1998. Stunning visual images help illustrate the worldwide diversity of eagles.

44

## Acknowledgments

Mike Allen, New York Department of Environmental Conservation

Chris Barone, U.S.D.A. Forest Service

Keith L. Bildstein, Hawk Mountain Sanctuary

Jed Burt, Ohio Wesleyan University

John Castrale, Indiana Division of Fish and Wildlife

David H. Ellis, Ph.D., Institute for Raptor Studies

Lynda J. Garrett, USGS Patuxent Wildlife Research Center

Cindy Hoffman, U.S. Fish and Wildlife Service

M. Alan Jenkins, George Miksch Sutton Avian Research Center

Sue Kirchoff, The Raptor Center—University of Minnesota

Mark Martell, The Raptor Center—University of Minnesota

Peter Nye, New York Department of Environmental Conservation

Mark C. Shieldcastle, Ohio Department of Natural Resources Division of Wildlife

Michael Whitecloud, Cheyenne and Arapaho Tribes of Oklahoma

Dr. John E. Becker writes children's books and magazine articles about nature and wild animals. He graduated from Ohio State University in the field of education. He has been an elementary school teacher, college professor, zoo administrator, and has worked in the field of wildlife conservation with the International Society for Endangered Cats. He currently lives in Delaware, Ohio, and teaches writing at the Thurber Writing Academy. He also enjoys visiting schools and sharing his love of writing with kids. In his spare time, Dr. Becker likes to read, hike in the woods, ice skate, and play tennis.